AF243962

# JUST DRIVE

# JUST DRIVE

Poems by Robert Cooperman

Cover art: "Taxi" © Michael Welply

Library of Congress Control Number: 2014936120
ISBN-13: 978-0-9898724-0-9

Published by Brick Road Poetry Press
P. O. Box 751
Columbus, GA 31902-0751
www.brickroadpoetrypress.com

Brick Road logo by Dwight New

My thanks to Charles Rammelkamp and to Rich Yurman for their spot-on comments and help with this collection in its earlier stages.

This book is for my brother Jeff, who knows because he drove; and also, as always, for my darling Beth.

# ACKNOWLEDGMENTS

Grateful acknowledgment is made to the editors of the publications in which these poems, some in earlier form, first appeared:

*Abbey*:  "Railroad Crossing Signs"
*Blue Collar Review*:  "My First Fare"
*Home Planet News*:  "Checker Cabs"
*Iodine Poetry Journal*:  "Cab Ride to Maimonides Hospital:  Brooklyn, New York"
*Misfit Magazine*:  "Robert Lowell in the Cab, I"
*Paterson Literary Review*:  "What Cabbies Knew"
*Snail Mail Review*:  "Mother and Daughter Fare"

# CONTENTS

# Why We Drove Cabs

For some guys—
and back in the Seventies
it was mostly guys—
driving was a way station
between acting gigs,
rock band tours,
before writing careers
took off like Daedalus,
before grad school in a state
so far away I'd fantasize
the fare to drive there.

A way to pay the bills
for guys laid off,
or whose small businesses
were caught by bankruptcy
like mice in hawks' talons:
temporary nests until
we could decide
about the rest of our lives.

But for lifers hacking paid
for their kids' education;
they retired to Florida
at the end of a shift
lasting thirty, forty years:
to play pinochle and brag
about epic fares;
to feel the thrum of engines,
the jolt of shock absorbers
shaky as medical skeletons
with every pothole;

to smell gas fumes
even while slicing
Thanksgiving turkeys
or shoveling in delectable
bacon and eggs.

New York's gasoline streets
forever ground into their sinuses,
forever part of their souls.

# The Names We Went By

"Cab driver," "Cabbie,"
"Taxi driver," or just "Taxi!"
arm raised, fingers snapping
to be taken somewhere important,
because they were,
which brings me back to
"Taxi Driver," as in the movie
that gave us all a bad name.

Also "Hack," short for "Hackney,"
the horse-drawn cab
of London's Victorian-sinister streets,
Sherlock Holmes shouting to hacks,
"Don't spare the horses!"
to avert a crime
or chase down a criminal.

And my favorite,
the one I confess to coining,
but so did every other hack
driven cynical by New York's
screaming streets:

"Yellow Cab Cowboy,"
cabbies slapping leather
to round up fares, to head off
cattle stampedes in our rush
to drop off fares
and rope other doggies,

then bragging 'round
the Belmore Cafeteria's campfire

or the sparse warmth of the bench
at our garage while we waited for cabs:

Yellow-Cab-Cowboy-Cabbie-Hack-
Taxi Driver, or just, "Hey you!"

## Taking the Hack Test

It wasn't like the test
for London cabbies
in their gondola-black cabs
on episodes of *Masterpiece Theatre*
or in films about World War II;
nothing close to as rigorous
as studying and driving
London's labyrinthine streets
for six months.

If you could read,
the garage sponsoring you
gave you the ten answers:
landmarks so famous
even visitors from Utah
knew how to find them:

Yankee Stadium,
Madison Square Garden,
Radio City, Carnegie Hall,
and six more everyone
in the world wanted to see.

I took the test
then was unleashed
onto New York's streets.

Poor New York.

# My First Fare

Four Cleveland conventioneers,
their combined girths groaning
the cab's shocks like rhinos,
their wedding bands digging
into the folds of fat on their fingers,
nudging each other that, "Hey,
we're really in New York:
sex everywhere for the grabbing."

"Where to?" I asked, trying to sound
enthusiastic as a flight attendant.

"Where can we get laid, kid?"
one of them demanded:  not
a trace of irony in his voice.

"How the hell should I know?"
I wanted to spit, but reminded
myself my job was just to drive,
so I answered, polite as apple sauce,

"How about Times Square?"
That block infamous, back then,
for hookers, pimps, pushers, and junkies:
all hungry as vampires, zombies,
and werewolves and twice as ferocious.

The four Musketeers happily agreed,

and I felt like a veteran hack
after five minutes behind the wheel;
felt too, the smallest twinge of pity

for them, but figured they were old
enough to know what they were getting into,
not to mention how to explain themselves
to their wives when their escapade
leaked out, and it was sure to.

# Between Careers

Like a lot of guys my age,
I was between careers: namely,
between being fired and grad school
in the fall, in the real America
far to the west of New York.

And all that was required
was a driver's license, a garage
to sponsor me, and enough English
to read the exam, the answers supplied.

My brother put in a word at his garage,
I had a driver's license, and since
I'd be studying Literature, I assured
the dispatcher I could read well enough
to pass the test and decipher street signs.

I further assured him I wasn't violent
or using drugs, though the last
a tiny white lie: for the reefer
I smoked when I could get some.

I won't say the money rolled in,
like in the old, bawdy song,
but I paid rent, utilities, and food,
got to a few movies, and even
saved a bit for autumn,

when I could escape New York,
in my own season of sweet mists.

## The Order of March

I picked up my cab at the garage
on West 57th and Eleventh,
between three and three-thirty,
and dove east.  Unless a fare
raised an arm, I'd take the right
onto Fifth, drive south in the far
left lane, until I got hailed.

Still empty, I'd make a left
just below 42nd, and another
onto Madison, and head north again,
and if still no luck, turn left
above 57th, left again onto Fifth,
and repeat the march, until a fare
gave me a destination, and a new route:
like joining the design-dots
on a HoJo's place-mat for kids.

Some cabbies lived and died
by airport fares, but before six,
easier, especially in rain or snow,
to trawl Midtown:  drifting west
or farther east when the fashionable
Fifth-Madison trade dried up,
dropping off fares fast as a Vegas dealer.

Around eight, dinner break;
with my brother or alone with a burger
and fries, digesting the sports section.

Then I'd stalk the Theatre District,

or the big hotels, to catch an airport fare,
and a fare (you never, ever wanted
to ride empty from the airports)
back to Manhattan, and clock out,
then trudge to the subway and home:
the line of march automatic, unthinking
as draftees calling out,

"Here, sergeant!" at roll call.

# Marilyn Monroe in a Cab

An older friend smiles
sly as a burlesque barker,
to tell of the time he tried
hailing a cab on Fifth Avenue:
women stalking, panther sleek;
men debonair as foxes.
And every cab in Manhattan full.

So, when a taxi finally screeched
to a stop, not five feet from Ted's
raised and pleading arm, and a woman
strangely familiar paid off the hack,
Ted gasped, dawning on him
with the force of Homer's sunrises,

that the passenger was Marilyn Monroe
without her makeup, looking
like she'd had a rough night,
and that Joltin' Joe might really
have belted her around a bit,
but still those legs, those breasts,
the jeans she was poured into.

Ted held his breath
as if his head was shoved underwater.

Walking past him, Marilyn smiled,
in role as an incognito Cleopatra
condescending to a commoner.

And while Ted was mesmerized

by her undulating wake, another
guy darted into the cab,
Marilyn vanishing.

# The Taxi Rules

You didn't ever hit a passenger,
you didn't ever demand a tip,
you didn't ever not take a fare
to a dangerous neighborhood,
you didn't ever take a fare off-meter:
otherwise known as theft.

In the case of a flat tire—
all too frequent because tires
were balder than my sweet
Uncle Charlie's bowling-ball skull—
you called for a replacement:
there was never a spare in the trunk;
partly, to save space for luggage,
partly, you could disarm the meter,
by some method I never figured out.

A front-ender?
You were suspended for a month,
because you were tailgating,
even if you weren't:
suspension hitting our wallets
like hammer-wielding Angels
who raged that our driving down
their East Village block was an act of war.

But lots of hacks didn't mind:
spent their days at the track,
or watching the Mets lose another:
more fun than sitting trapped
in the rush-hour war.

# The War Lover

He shouted an address
and assured me, loudly,
the country was going to hell,

"With all these hippie-traitors,"
apparently not noticing my pony tail
or beard, assuming I was an honest
working stiff, like himself.

"Who do you like in the Series?"
I tried to break his flow of bile,
but he talked over me, asserting,

"We got to get behind the President
and support the War, or you and me
will be speaking Russian and Chinese,
not to mention whatever lingo
the Vietcong  jabbers."

I prayed—a little kid who had to pee—
I could drop him at his destination,
before we'd start shouting, or worse:
me New York's most hostile pacifist.

But the light was broken, or a malevolent
god was playing tricks with the signal.

"You just get back from Nam?" I interrupted.
"Have a son in harm's way?" remembering
my poor friend Mark's mother,
who, when we sat shiva with her, told me,
"Don't go, Bobby, no matter what!"

Silence fell in my cab, heavy as incoming
artillery; the light finally green.
He didn't leave a tip:  the silence,
like calming Northern Lights, enough.

## Cab Ride to Maimonides Hospital:
## Brooklyn, New York

Right after I drop one fare
at an Upper West Side apartment house,
a guy runs for my cab as if chased by Angels.

"Maimonides Hospital!" he shouts.
"Take the Tunnel." I glance back at him
as we rocket down to Brooklyn.
He sits sobbing, "It's my Dad!"

And I'm back at that night not so long
before: the phone call, the frantic cab ride,
my shrieking-realization halfway
downtown that my father was dead,
the driver handing me a smoke,
a calming pint of scotch:
talking as if to a kid terrified
on speed and the knife in his hand.

"It'll be all right," I assure the guy,
knowing it probably won't be.
"My Dad had three scares and was fine
after each one," I lie: the memory
of his going still raw as a steak
slapped over a fist-fight black eye.

But I talk and talk: my voice gentle
as we blast down Fort Hamilton Parkway.
He tosses me a bill, and gallops
for the Emergency Entrance.

And I recall the long, slow drive
to the morgue later that morning,
my father lying on a gurney,
not looking anything like asleep.

## Boxing Out

On two-way streets, the idea
was to ride the right-hand lane,
like boxing out for a rebound.
I was cruising Central Park West,
the cab to my left trying to cut me off,
when a fare flagged me, my rival's horn
a flock of indignant geese.

He kept loud-and-cursing pace,
and when we stopped at the next light,
spat tobacco-juice invectives.
Finally, my passenger rolled down
his window, and leaning out,
purred to the other cabbie,

"You know, I'm a bit of a psychic."

"So who gives a flying shit?"
the cabbie shouted.

"Well," my man conversed, convivial
as a boulevardier.  "I can tell
that in ten seconds, you're going
to get out of your cab, and on your knees
you'll apologize to this nice gentleman."

When my passenger pulled out a gun,
its muzzle wider than fieldpieces
at Gettysburg, on the one hand,
I silently chortled to see a bully reduced
to pissing himself on his knees;

on the other hand, a guy sitting behind me
was armed more heavily than Doc Holliday.

"You can't let assholes jerk you around, kid,"
he holstered his cannon, and we rode out.

# End of Shift

By the time I delivered my cab
back to my garage, I could've kissed
the gasoline-slick, paper-chewing-gum-
strewn, and coffee-slithery floor,
in thanks that I hadn't killed anyone
on New York's very hostile streets.

Along Midtown avenues,
all civility and traffic lanes vanished:
more like buffalo stampedes,
along with my shouted wish
to vaporize every vehicle and moron
pedestrian who thought jaywalking
Fifth Avenue in rush hour
was a country path stroll.

Then the fares:  spitting destinations,
informing me how much, exactly.
the ride should cost, as if I'd ripped
them off before I'd started the meter;
or the ones not sure where they wanted
to go, so I drove around and around
while they decided on the address,
as if torn between onion and sesame bagels,
nova scotia lox or white fish salad.

And throw in the headache-heat,
the kids who bolted without paying,
my right ankle throbbing from
the gas-brake-gas-brake cha-cha.

So yes, I was tempted to kiss
the garage floor, except I knew
I'd have to do it over again next night.

# The Jousting Shield

You know how, at Medieval Fairs
and movies about the Age of Chivalry,
when actors playing knights joust,
and shields shatter with a lance's impact?

That's how a door exploded
when the driver opened it without looking:
a guy from my garage steaming down
Seventh Avenue by the Garden-Penn Station,
in search of a fare, the way knights
rode down opponents, lances extended.

Frank's cab flew like a helmet plume,
the other car's door blasted off its hinges,
the driver diving back into his car,
Frank screeching into the underground garage:
to survey the damage and wait out the cops,
and in Frank's mind,
"The douchebag had it coming,
for not paying attention."

By a miracle, only one headlight shattered;
Frank figured he could claim a vandal
had smashed it with a hammer
while he'd stopped for dinner.

And that's exactly what he said,
and none of us dared rat him out
to the dispatcher:  all of us guilty
of something like it, one time or another.

## Checker Cabs

Boxes on wheels, but nothing
on Manhattan's streets could run
with them for a block or so:  not
muscle cars, not Corvettes, not Ferraris,
let alone our garage's plodding Dodges
when the light drag-raced green
and we floored it to screech first
in front of raised-arm fares.

Checkers were the quarter horses
of the taxi world:  lightning
on four tires, and oh, I wished
our garage would switch its fleet:
not just to compete for fares,
but sweet nostalgia—for when
I was a kid, and our parents took
my brother and me into Manhattan
to dinner and a Broadway play once,
and decided to splurge on a cab.

Jeff and I rode on those fold-down
jumper seats facing our parents,
a thrill greater than the exotic City:
something on the order of blasting off
with Flash Gordon and Buck Rogers,
Jeff and me working our invisible
control panels to send us into orbit,

while our parents conversed
in whispered intimacies, looked up,
smiled, and shook their heads

at their cockamamie sons:  both
of whom would one day dream
of driving Checker Cab spaceships.

## The Five-Dollar Tip

Elegant as Jackie O, she hailed my cab.
Neither of us attempted conversation:
me shell-shocked from cacophonies
of traffic homicidal as heavy artillery;
she in a world where cabbies were holdovers
from coachmen snapping whips at fours-in-hand.

She gave me a sawbuck for the ride,
and when I handed back a five and three singles,
she handed me the fin for a tip, thanked me
in a voice of polite patrician distance,
and flew into an office building.

"Ma'am," I called out. "Ma'am!"
but she'd vanished, that five
burning its guilt into my hand.

I drove off, vowing to give the Abe
to the first homeless squeegee guy I saw.
But none of those wraiths materialized,
and that bill hissed,

"I'm yours, kid. You earned me."

# An Analogy

In my cab, I'd think of myself
as a combination pimp-prostitute:
picking up riders,

dropping them off, taking their fares
and tips—a sort of fair trade—
then finding the next ride.

No bodily fluids were exchanged,
and instead of women asking,
"Hey honey, you want a date?"

fares would raise an arm,
whistle like incoming missiles.
It wasn't the sweaty and old—

men and women with canes,
shaking hands, and metronoming
heads—I held in contempt,

but the young and healthy,
who talked about nothing
but themselves, and never said,

"Hello, how are you today?"
when they got in and gave me
an address:  unwilling

to walk five blocks on sunny
Fifth Avenue, since, of course,

they owned the world,

and had paid for my services.

# Taxi Driver

Remember the De Niro movie?
Remember the garage—grimy
as a Bowery flophouse—
and the brief shot of the dispatcher,
his body lumpy as a sack of laundry,
his voice raspy as a Marlboro milkshake,
growling the names of cabbies
into a microphone, dispensing cabs
like cards at stud poker?

That was the garage I drove for,
the dispatcher, who doled out cabs
with brakes vaporized in acid baths,
shocks shaky as five-day-bender drunks,
half hoping we'd fatally front-end.

If we didn't yell, "Here!" fast and loud
as political prisoners at roll call, he'd shout,
"Greene, you scumbag, you want a cab
or not!"  Or "Cooperman, you useless
pissant, answer at your name,
or I'll give you a cab condemned
before Moses parted the freakin' Red Sea."

To say he was a piece of shit
was to insult that bodily function.
He started us down the road of rage
so common to driving a cab
in New York City's Rush Hour.

"Fuck you, asshole!" we yelled
as we pulled out of the garage
and into traffic, and woe
to any driver who got in our way.

# Here's How It Worked

We hoped for cabs with brakes
a little less mushy than oatmeal,
shocks that didn't buck like Brahma bulls,
and headlights that didn't fade and die
like torches in a cave in a horror movie.

We handed our hack licenses to the dispatcher;
he chose who got which cab:  part seniority,
part guys telling him jokes, part how much
and how discreetly he'd been bribed.

We had to record each fare on a log sheet:
where we picked them up, where we dropped
them off, and how much on the meter.
There was a metal strongbox that could be opened
only with a key we were never given;
into it we were supposed to stash every bill
and coin, but guys used pockets, cigar boxes.

At shift's end, we handed every meter-penny
to the guy who counted the take:  half
to the garage; half, minus taxes, to the driver,
which amounted to about a third.
Loose change the counter kept, as a tip.

There were ways to cheat the garage,
but most of us just wanted to finish our shifts
and fall into bed; too tired to sort the tip-coins
into our wine bottles for jingling accumulations.
So we'd wake with change strewn all over our beds—
metal crumbs from metal pizzas—
before we had to groan up and ride again.

# Moon Over Sixth Avenue

I'd dropped an elderly couple
in the West Village; they'd bickered
all the way from Brooklyn,
as if dueling with pinking shears.
They turned their cutting edges at me
when I announced the bill at ride's end:
common enemies the key
to their happy-ever-after marriage.

Trying to breathe, I headed up Sixth,
and almost crashed my cab,
not from still hearing their barbs,
but suspended between skyscrapers
the jolly butter glow of the full moon,
so low and huge in the sky it might
be an alien spaceship offering us all
one last chance of living in peace.

And though fares were fighting
for empty cabs, I pulled over:  to watch
that globe famed for blessing lovers,
as that pair must've been once;
and also to breathe the moon's stillness.

It ascended like a balloon slipping
from a child's greasy grip, taking
its magic with it, until it was time
to drive again:  leopard-alert for people
in a hurry, and no patience
for the vanishing magic of the full moon.

# Losing My Brakes on Columbus Avenue

If the dispatcher wanted to screw you,
he gave you a cab with an oil leak,
or with belts about to Frisbee off,
or tires so bald you'd blow one,
and have to wait for a replacement,
all the time losing precious fares.

But if he really wanted to screw you,
he turned murderous:  like the time
Stan gave me a cab with brakes
held together with bubble gum,
mucilage, and muttered prayers,
for talking back the day before,
over something I'd forgotten,
but Stan forgot nothing, held grudges
like the Rockefeller Center statue
of Atlas holding up the globe.

Off I went with brakes mushier
than mashed potatoes, dropped off
one fare, another, a third, and was about
to pick up a fourth at Columbus and 76th,
a steady drizzle auguring business
and tips that might set records—

when the brakes failed; I rammed
my foot at the emergency brake,
and aimed for a street sign pole,
thankful uphill inertia taking over.
And to make sure, I slashed
the transmission into "Park,"

the cab bucking like a clown's barrel
smacked by a Brahma bull
at the just-ended stock-show-rodeo.

Sweaty, shaking, my mouth
too frightened-dry to curse, I trudged off
to find a pay phone:  not quite dumb
enough to think about revenge.

# Games of Scrabble

Some nights—or mornings—
when I'd drag in from my nightshift cab,
I'd be greeted by my insomniac neighbor,
waiting with the Scrabble board set up,
a couple of beers, and herbal comfort.

Without a word, we'd sit down to play,
me wired from driving all over Manhattan
and everywhere else fares demanded
to be taken, Vic just wired:

"I haven't had a decent night's sleep
since 1965," he once half-joked,
looked like a vampire minus the fangs,
and usually beat me as if English
were my third, very shaky language.

We set down tiles, toted up our scores,
sipped beer, and smoked; my whole body
vibrating from the cellular memory
of the cab's motion, my right ankle
gnawed by small, vicious rodents
from the gas-brake-gas-brake stomp,
and sleep a hypothetical concept
for which there was absolutely no proof.

Brushing my teeth before I left for work,
I'd stare at a face growing pale as Vic's.

# Nightshift

Most cabbies wanted nightshift:
more street trade, better tips,
and no getting up at 3:30 AM.

You had to average forty bucks
on the meter per hundred miles
to keep that status, which back
in the early Seventies meant a frenzy
of pick-ups, drop-offs, and maybe
a half hour for dinner at eight or so:
the streets dead, fares
already where they wanted to be.

Plus you had to keep the cab out
at least nine hours,
which some cabbies got around
by taking only airport trade,
and sleeping on line waiting
for the next Midtown fare.

In theory, you couldn't deny
anyone or any neighborhood,
but most hacks would flip
the "Off-Duty" sign if they were hailed
by any guy who wasn't white,
even in a suit natty as Cary Grant,
even if he was Harry Belafonte
standing with Bill Cosby,
Walt Frazier, Ralph Bunch,
and Frederick Douglass.

Nightshift meant hobbling home
between one and two, exhausted,
wired like a bomb, so you'd read
or work the Sunday crossword,
and curse and curse and hurl
the magazine section across the room
like a startled seagull:  daylight
starting to gray the insomniac sky.

## Three Kids in the Back Seat

After a Knicks game at the Garden,
three kids crowded into my backseat,
and gave me an address somewhere
in the rat's maze of where the West Village
labyrinths into Little Italy, and back again.

They laughed and shouted and, as
we used to say in Brooklyn, ranked
each other out about the relative merits
of their mothers in hypothetical beds.

But nothing with real imagination
or the bile that might require fists and blood,
just friends flying on a rare Knicks win,
and from weed and beers.

On one dim red-stoplight corner,
the doors flew open, and out they ran:
laughing, punching each other,
flipping me the bird with both hands,
and disappearing into an alleyway,
kicking over garbage cans in their glee.

Muttering, I slammed the gaping doors,
admitted that if I were completely honest,
I'd have been tempted to do likewise:
if I were with friends, our spirits high
on reefer, brews, a hometown win,
and invincible, immortal youth.

# The Chess Players at the Taxi Garage

We staggered in for our shift,
handed the dispatcher
our laminated hack licenses,
and waited on the bench splintery
as a shattered baseball bat.

I read, another guy worked
crossword puzzles, a third played
his flute until the dispatcher shouted,

"Shut up, you hippie asshole!
I can't hear myself think."
What Stan had to think about—
aside from how to screw us—
none of us could figure out.

Two guys hunched over
their chessboard when I arrived,
the same Rodin pose
when I returned my cab at night:
always concentrating on the board:
hypnotic to watch them performing
their minimalist dance of moving a piece,
maybe taking an opponent's piece,
the game never-ending:

two middle-aged Thinkers:
one hand holding up a jaw,
the other poised like a cobra,
like a scene from Bergman's

masterpiece, *The Seventh Seal*,
the Dispatcher our angel of death,
handing us death-trap cabs.

# The Streets at Night:  Winter

At a certain time of night
almost every corner of Midtown
is adorned by a shivering woman

in hot pants, earrings that dangle
like wind chimes, and heels Babel-high.
In a way, we're in similar businesses:

only bodily fluids are seldom exchanged
in my cab, and I've less to worry about:
with the Plexiglas separator a spate of murders

finally moved the Taxi Board to order
installed:  to protect hacks from guys my Dad
carried a wrench for when he'd been fired

from safer jobs, and drove a cab.
When I trawl the streets for fares,
I see those ladies standing, dancing

leg to leg to keep the cold at bay without
the fires Rome's prostitutes build for warmth,
and symbols of the flames they'll light in men.

I shiver in sympathy in my warm cab,
and curse the fares at movies, the ballet,
the theatre, or swanky restaurants;

or staying home this freezing night.
Time, I rationalize, to turn in my cab:
one lady always stands by the subway

entrance; we've gotten to the stage
of intimacy that I nod at her, and she's
stopped asking if I want a date.

# The Streets at Night:  Summer

The season every hack dreaded,
sweat smearing foreheads and arms,
hands slick as snail slime on steering wheels,

curses a worry-bead litany exploding
more emphatic than Ahab
be-damning the White Whale:

and not a fare to drag into the backseat,
everyone walking for once in their lives.
Only the drivers who sucked up

to Stan the dispatcher rode air-conditioned cabs.
Otherwise, we rolled down windows
and hoped our few fares weren't homicidal

maniacs when they got out of the cab,
and instead of handing us some bills,
pulled a gun or knife on a deserted block

of window-shot-out factories and weed-
and-broken-bottle choked lots quieter
than dusty Old West ghost towns.

Those nights I'd hang out at the airports
or the Pierre or Plaza; or if I got lucky
with a fare to Yankee Stadium or Shea,

I'd spring for a bleacher seat,
and take a happy-soused fan to Midtown,

and he'd not puke all over the backseat,

while breezes cooled the long, hot day.

# Snow Cab

It was going to be the night's last fare,
when snow started to fling down
like the dumping maws of a million backhoes,
and I was about to tell the young couple
who had just jumped into my cab—
brushing snow from their shoulders
and shivering in the sudden warmth—

I had to go off-duty: the streets too slick,
my tires bald as boiled eggs.
But I feared they'd both sob in desperation,
so cold—snow a billion stinging shards—
I reassured them we'd take the ride
slow and steady as a snow-cat.

As I inched onto the East Side Highway,
the tires splayed like a skater sprawled
on an iced-over lake, the cab spun,
the couple screamed, and my panicked hands
steered, praying not to hit anything.

We came to a halt inches from the guardrail,
with nothing barreling down on us.

"You were great, man," he enthused.
"Wonderful," his pretty friend agreed,
and smiled as if she'd kiss me;
he smiled too, as if he wouldn't mind.

We crawled along, the wiper blades
clattering faster than the cab:

neither of them with a clue how lucky
we'd all been, and still, the long,
treacherous drive through the enemy
territory of falling snow.

# Sid the Hack

While we hacks waited for our cabs,
he'd boast he'd been a pro boxer,
flicking left-right combos,
though his gut got in the way.

"After that, I was a bagman
for the mob, but my Ma made me
promise on her deathbed,
that I'd find honest work."

By honest, Sid meant the time
he'd picked up a drunk out-of-towner
at Kennedy, who slurred he had to be
at Newark for another flight,
then lapsed into snoring
loud enough to awaken all the guys
who'd died in cab backseats
while doing the dirty deed
with women young enough
to be their sexy nieces.

Sid claimed he'd dropped the guy
at another JFK terminal, and pocketed
the out-of-state fare and a tip
big enough to make a mob boss happy
with his collection techniques.

He told that story so often I just read—
until the time he loomed over me, grabbed
*Crime and Punishment*, and sneered,
"I'll teach you to freakin' not listen."

I sat staring, torn between wanting
to shove the ripped pages down his throat
and knowing if I even thought about it
for another second, he'd beat me silly;
and knew with even more certainty, none
of the other hacks would lift a finger.

# Nicci the Cabdriver

In her ponytail, Harris-wool cap,
men's faded work shirts, and frame
lanky as a champion miler, she waited
for her cab with the rest of us,
and wrote in a marbled notebook:
the only woman at our garage.

We never asked what she was writing:
partly her aura of indifferent disdain;
partly the shepherd-mix monster
at her feet:  force fields to stop us all.

Except Sid, and his bottomless
pint of rye, his fists big and hard
as bear traps, and his swagger.
On Nicci's first day,
he started to lean over her,
his hand reaching to cop a feel,
when her pen pressed against his throat,
her dog's guard hairs like the spiked
collars of medieval mastiffs.

The rest of us silently cheered;
after that, he'd snarl, but never to her face,
"The bitch likes dogs more than men."

We never said a word in her defense:
not that she needed, or wanted, our gallantry.

# Waiting for Cabs

When we waited for cabs,
Sid couldn't keep his mouth shut,
his stories more and more outrageous:
like the time he hit an old lady,
his cab's front fender scooping her
like a cow catcher, sending her flying.

"The old bitch," he laughed, "should've
stayed home, not tried to cross the street."

And when I failed to laugh with him,
he threatened to beat me so black and blue,

"Your mother won't recognize you!"
knowing I'd cower like an omega wolf:
except this time.  Without thinking, I spat,

"But your mother does, every time."

"You're freakin' dead meat!" he roared,
his fist raised to splatter me, cabbies gathering:
enjoying the spectacle of someone else
getting smacked like a punching bag—
when Stan the dispatcher, croaked,

"This ends now.  Shake hands,
or neither of you drives in New York again."

The next afternoon, word whispered
that Sid had had a mild heart attack;

other hacks stared as if I'd shoved him
under an oncoming D Train, and trod
a wide circle around my black magic mojo.

# Robert Lowell in the Cab, I

He was fleeing his third wife,
Caroline Blackwood, for his second,
Elizabeth Hardwick, and clutching
the Lucien Freud portrait
of the young Blackwood,
when the heart attack felled him
like a careless logger flattened
by a toppled redwood.

One can only speculate on why
he was carrying that painting
while returning to the woman
he'd spurned in the first place:

But I always felt lucky
no one died in my backseat.
The closest?  The woman
who groaned to lower
her old bones, while she held
an urn:  its contents obvious.

She set the urn beside her
and announced her destination;
and since she kept silent about
her companion, so did I.

When we pulled up to the address,
she paid and left without the urn.

"Ma'am," I called, trying to put
as much kindness into my callow voice

as I could.  "You forgot something."

She waved me off and kept walking.

# Ladies of the Backseat

Two halter-topped,
hot-panted, stiletto-heeled
ladies dove into my cab,
and told me to drive
around and around the block.

Their faces hidden,
I couldn't tell
if they were beautiful
or barbed-wire hard.

But their hair was blonde
and elaborate:  announcing
men had maligned Medusa
for far too long.

They stared out their windows
for guys who looked like
vice-cops, which I'd no idea
how to identify:  innocent
as a kid from Wisconsin.

We circled and circled:
Times Square blaring
like flocks of geese.
Finally, they had me stop.

"We're sorry, kid, we ain't
got nothing for a tip," one said,
and leaned in to hand me the bills
and coins, and for a crazy

instant I thought she'd kiss me
and tell me I was sort of cute.

# The Ride He Still Talks About

While we waited for cabs
one afternoon, a guy fidgeted
like his bladder would burst.

"What?" I finally demanded;
he poured the tale:  two actresses,
famous for what we called "Art films,"
got into his cab, flirty as Mae West,
and invited him up to their apartment,
where—and here he sputtered
and turned red as movie-magic blood—
he whispered the particulars.

I stared.  He was less sexy
than Wally Cox in the *Mr. Peepers*
TV series about the diminutive,
mild-as-cornflakes sleuth.

Still, he'd lived—maybe in fantasy,
maybe for real—the dream
every hack held more dear
than finding a sack engorged
with too many hundred-dollar bills
to count in a double-shift night.

# The Man with a Cat

So thin, I hardly noticed he'd sat down,
except he was clutching a cat fatter
than Carroll's Cheshire, but not a smile
on its girth, as it settled onto his lap,
and he fed it treats from a cornucopia pocket.

"Know why I feed Skeeter so well?"

"Okay, why?"  I asked:  he was paying
for the ride, thus entitled to talk non-stop.

"So he won't eat me should I have a coronary
or stroke, gasping in my pee and poop.

"Also," he smirked at superior knowledge
when I glanced into the crazed mirror,
"if I keep feeding him, he'll go before me,
so problem solved," his logic airtight
as rooms in old Saturday matinee serials,
their walls crushing closer and closer
until the stalwart hero and plucky heroine
were pulverized into an ooze of red jelly,

except, they always escaped.

# The Actress

She was a once celebrated
British actress with drunken eyes
of blue; she slurred the address,
like her tongue was brittle
as a stick of ancient chewing gum.

"57th Street and Madison,
you grotty little git!" she roared,
and named a famous hotel,
so I punched the meter and hit
every pothole on Sixth Avenue:
not the wisest way to get even,
since she might've puked
all over the backseat
and the Plexiglas divider.

As I was about to slide
into the right turn onto 57th,
she screamed, "Left, left, you idiot!
*West 57th* and Madison!"

"Lady," my turn to spit,
"there is no West 57th and Madison."
Her silence a stalking leopard.

Two minutes later, she wobbled
from the cab:  a little girl
in her mother's high heels.

"The fare's $3.50," I shouted,

She waved a dismissive hand,
and the doorman shrugged,

"What can you do, kid?"

# The Celebrity

Aside from the actress drunk
and vicious as the 16th century
Hungarian princess, Elizabeth Bathoray,
who bathed in the blood
of murdered virgins:  hoping
she'd live forever young,

a national TV network anchorman
was the closest I ever came
to a celebrity riding in my cab.

Unfortunately, when he sat down
and smiled, waiting for the moment
of double-take recognition,
I'd forgotten his name.

His anticipation withered;
his eyes, in my rearview, lost
their sparkle, as if I'd robbed him
at gun point; he asked a few questions,
so maybe I'd recognize his voice,
which I did, and he seemed affable
enough, and not at all full of himself.
But I'd be damned and dazed
if I could recall his name.

At the TV studio, he limped, defeated, out
to marveling stares and swiveling heads;
tourist cameras snapped and snapped;
a couple ran over for autographs;

a few people shot him a thumbs-up
for his courageous reporting on the War:
his steps lighter, a touch more swagger
in his stride as he entered the building.

And still, I couldn't remember his name.

# The Assassin

His shirt torn, his hair a tornado-
ripped wheat field, he raised his arm,
and maybe I should've kept driving,
but I never passed up a fare, unless
he was wielding a gun or chain saw.

He gave a Williamsburg address,
and it was then I saw the blood
seeping like sewer water from one arm;
he cradled the limb like a tiny baby.

"We've got to get you to a hospital,"
my voice a helium-filled balloon.

"No!" he groaned, pain replacing
the numb shock that had gotten him
as far as my cab.  "Get me home;
my old lady knows what to do."

I could feel his watching eyes
when we passed a cop car and I didn't
signal trouble was riding in my backseat.

"Thanks," he whispered.  "I owe you."

Finally, the trip over, he shoved a Capone-
extravagant tip and business card at me.

"If you ever need anyone taken
care of, I never forget a kindness."

His card singed my fingers,

the back seat suddenly empty,
my "Off-Duty" sign well-lit,
the cab's doors safely locked.

## "My Wife Left Me"


"My wife left me," he sobbed,
collapsed into my backseat.
"Just drive, I don't care where!"

Through Central Park, up
the Westside Highway to the Cloisters,
back down again, the meter ticking
every tenth of a mile:  my dream ride,
except the poor guy was crying,
gasping as if from an asthma attack,
begging his absent wife,

"What did you want?  What could've
I have done different?  Why did you
have to fall for that schmuck?
Why can't we go back to what we had?"

Finally, I said, "You got anyplace
you want to go?"  The hour, as Dylan sang,
getting late:  almost time for the shift change.

"No, just keep driving."

I sighed and the meter ticked
like the clock inside the crocodile
hunting Captain Hook.  And suddenly,
he was asleep:  mouth open, face smudged.

He came to, wild-eyed, as if I'd left him—
for dead—in a Jersey swamp, and groaned,

"Take me home, I got no place else to go,"
or I might still be driving him.

64

# Weekend Driving

We had to give the garage
one night a weekend;
I slept Sundays and Mondays,
drove Saturdays:  singles
and couples hopping from bars
to parties:  tips like wind-driven
October leaves.

One Saturday, an affable couple
invited me to a party.
I'd made my quota, so figured
what the hell, and met a too-young
widow:  her husband a much older,
famous painter:  a loving genius.
She shook herself, and smiled,

"Tell me about yourself."

I shrugged that I'd be leaving
soon for a Denver grad school.

"The Great American West,"
she smiled sadly, and we talked
literature.  When I told her
I had to get the cab to the garage,
but was free later, she kissed
my cheek, sweaty from gasoline streets,
dismissing my young, young hope
for a happy ending.

## Dinner Breaks

The nights my brother and I drove,
we'd scarf dinner at a Burger & Brew:
a chain gone the way of Stone Age fires.

The first few times, we discussed
the Knicks:  in the twilight glow
of their glory days; or movies;
or what we'd be doing for fun.

After a few nights—backs aching,
heads spinning, ankles throbbing—
our conversations degenerated
into where we picked up fares,
where we dropped them off,
and how much of a tip they left:
cursing cheap bastards in ever-rising
crescendos of four-letter invention.

Soon we excised all verbs, used only
the proper nouns of streets, avenues,
airports, the Garden, hospitals;
we lobbed expletive grenades
while we downed burgers and fries,
snarling like wolves:  mad to earn
enough to call it an early night,
and do something besides drive and sleep.

# The Belmore Cafeteria

On Park Avenue South and E. 29<sup>th</sup>,
it was the cabbies' clubhouse,
where we could bullshit about the lousy
street trade and eat a meal any time
of the day and most of the night.

Old hacks presided like crime bosses
regaling younger cabbies with tales
of out-of-town, thousand-buck fares
at the pleading of babes dressed only
in mink coats, diamond necklaces,
and lust for cab drivers:
the universal cabbie fantasy,

"Before De Niro ruined it for us,
in that piece of shit flick I couldn't watch.
And if the putz ever shows his face
in here, I'll kick his ass to Times Square,
for the pimps to carve him up good,"
one old timer intoned every time
enough guys gathered to listen,

as if we'd hunkered by flickering
cowboy campfires, when talk
turned to tales of epic cattle drives
and heroic Indian-fighting.

# Driving on St. Patrick's Day

Aside from New Year's Eve,
it was the best night of the year
to drive a New York City cab.

Like the ads for Levy's Real Jewish Rye,
you didn't need to be Irish to frolic
on that most rambunctious of holy nights.

Drinking started early, with the parade
that danced past the Cathedral named
for the saint:  a dour-faced teetotaler.

Then there was the elderly couple,
too hammered to stagger from their bar
to their apartment in Inwood Hill:

far above the more fashionable Manhattan.
His fingers shook to hand me a ten-spot.
"Keep the change," he slurred

when I helped them to the curb.
She fell, her knees seeping; he fell too.
I took their hands as if Hansel and Gretel,

lost and frightened in the witch's forest,
and fit their key into their lock.  He tried
to hand me another ten and proclaimed,

"Yer a gentleman and a scholar," when I refused
and shook his hand, let his wife kiss

my cheek, stroke my face, and call me,

"Grand, good boy.  Stay this way forever."

# Mother and Daughter Fare

An older woman and her adult daughter
groan into my cab at a Park Avenue doctor's office.

"Don't push me!" the old lady shrieks.
"You'll be rid of me soon enough
and have the life you whine about."

Her daughter sighs from the life of servitude
she's endured out of love and obligation.
I punch the meter, and we're off,
the dragon cataloguing her daughter's
many shortcomings in dress, manner, behavior,
and the men her mother has had to get rid of.

I worry how, exactly, she disposed of
those unsuitable suitors, as if I'm watching
a wizened, vicious Bette Davis movie.

Finally, we reach their destination;
the daughter pays, smiles as if to apologize
for what I've witnessed, and I help
the old lady from my cab, while she flirts,
tells me how I must make my mother proud,

"Even if you're not a doctor or lawyer,"
her digs a reflex; then she turns her cobra eye
on her daughter, whose eye I try to catch
as well, and, in my turn, silently apologize.

# Conspiratorial Tones

As a cowardly-lion,
I would allow myself to rave
at everyone and everything
only when my cab was empty
and I was wedged into lanes
and lanes of unmoving traffic
in Midtown Manhattan.

Except once, the fare hauling
himself into my backseat,
and immediately pointing
at the black cop directing traffic,
and in the tone of comfortable
conspirators, he launched into:

"Lookit.  Thinks he owns the city.
They're taking over, them
and the Ricans and the kikes,
and they ain't gonna leave
nothin' for nobody else."

At which point, my silent,
sputtering rage volcanoed into,

"Shut up, you ignorant piece
of racist shit!" I crushed
the brakes and ordered,
"Get out of my cab!"

"Well screw you for the fare!"
he shouted, slamming his door,
trying to yank mine open:

the time for bravery over, I locked
all the doors, shot him the bird,
and escaped around the corner.

# The Old Man and the Muggers

First thing you've got to know:
I'm a devout coward.
So it must've been a combination
of cheap passengers, blaring horns,
and being pissed-off at April's promise
of romance, and me a prisoner of my cab.

But when I saw two punks circling
an old man:  laughing, feinting with knives,
and no one doing a thing, I metamorphosed
into the Lone Ranger:  smacked one guy
from behind; when he went down,
I kicked and kicked him, though I'd never
done that violence to anyone before or since.

When the other one saw his partner rolled
into a fetal ball, he took off, like in cowboy
movies, when the bad guys figure the odds
are no longer in their murderous favor.

"You okay?" I asked the old man,
who was brushing off his black coat,
picking up his fedora and skullcap.
He nodded, dignity restored,
shook my hand in thanks, and asked,

"Young man, when was the last time
you laid *tefilin*?"  I sighed, his question
really, "Why aren't you a better Jew,

saying your prayers regularly?"

No good deed ever going unpunished.
At least no one had stolen my cab.

# Out-of-Town Fare

What I dreamed of:  a famous musician,
actor, or better, Bellow, Roth, Drabble, Oates,
or best of all, the ghost of Keats or Homer,
would sink into my backseat and declare,
"Take me to Montauk" or "New Haven."

Fares outside the City were double the meter,
some had to be negotiated, and the tips,
the tips!  Ali Baba's cave of jewels and gems.

That magic passenger would regale me
with stories, hand me joints, pastrami sandwiches,
tongue-biting Cokes, and advise, "Take your time."
Time, after all, merely an intellectual construct.

He'd quote from his greatest works,
favorite lines of poetry, ask what I was writing,
which back then, was nothing:  too wiped
and wired after driving to do anything
but smoke dope, play Scrabble, and sleep.

But of course, that out-of-town fare
remained a figment of wishes never
to be granted, but always dreamed of.

Just the grind down Fifth, up Madison,
over to Sixth, Broadway, to JFK, LaGuardia,
into Brooklyn, the Bronx, Queens's rat's maze,
then home, home, home:  to sleep, to dream.

# Off the Meter

We were all tempted to take fares off-meter,
instead of forking over half to the garage:
cabbies responsible for the tax, thus our take
sliced to one-third of the meter.
So the rationale:  we were getting even.

We could buy a switch to bypass the meter,
and make the "On-Duty" roof-light glow
as if the ride were legit.  But if the fare
was a hack inspector:  we'd be suspended,
fined, or fired faster than greyhounds
in futile pursuit of the steel jack-rabbit.

So I resisted that temptation.

One spring Saturday evening,
clocking out early for a party, I took a cab.
The hack, my age, asked if it was okay
to ride off-meter, and quoted a price:  trying
I knew, to rip me off like I was a civilian.

"Take it on the meter," I growled low and sinister
as Bogart, and told him, exactly, the route,
but didn't have the heart to stiff him for a tip
when we pulled up to the apartment house:
music throbbing, silhouettes dancing behind
the smoke-fluttering curtains of one apartment.

"Next time," I advised, "don't be so greedy,"
and felt tough and sexy as Jimmy Cagney
for the first and only time in my life.

# Black Widow

In a sable coat that rippled
in the backseat twilight,
she gave me the address:
her voice throaty as Bacall's,
but more dangerous,
for using her power over
poor schmucks who couldn't
keep their fevered eyes off her.

Like I was having trouble doing
while I navigated Manhattan.
At any instant, she'd reveal
she was wearing nothing under her fur,
except the sleek skin, sculpted
breasts, and sipping-spoon navel
that god—or the devil—
had given her in their bargain.

Her voice—half purr, half growl—
when she asked about me,
never revealing the least fact,
or lie, about herself.

By ride's end, I felt naked, sweaty:
her voice the flute that summons
the cobra, and the cobra's musical hiss.

And then she was gone.

# Smoking Dope

That black-hearted satirist,
Evelyn Waugh, might've called them
"Bright Young Things" as they tittered
into my backseat outside St. Patrick's Cathedral,
announcing they'd come from a wedding.

They gushed at what "a pig's dinner"
the bishop had made of the ceremony.

"Drunker than Mummy on a Sunday
afternoon of Daddy at the Club,"
she giggled, so we all knew, "The Club"
meant the old man's younger mistress.

Her companion declared the bride
and groom had been high on reefer;
to prove it, he lit a joint, asking me,

"You don't mind, do you?"
She took a hit, handed the joint back,
and sighed rueful apologies,

"We'd share, but it's all we have,"
while he rolled a fresh joint.

After I dropped them at an Upper East Side
address they could've walked to,
I aired out the cab:  not just the weed stink,
but even more, their odors of,

"Isn't it wonderful to be us!"

# Railroad Crossing Signs

Some nights, when fares
had vanished like taunting
ghosts of old lovers
I was too young to have had,
I'd be so crazed and desperate
for raised, signaling arms
and the fear that other cabbies
had stolen the passengers
that belonged, by right, to me,
I'd confuse the giant "X's"
of railroad crossing signs
for waiting fares.

I'd race for what I thought,
hoped, would be a ride
juicy as my poor man's T-bone—
a rare burger and fries—
to LaGuardia, JFK, or blessed
destination, out of state:
double the fare and tip;
only to behold my face and heart
falling like an angel
tossed from heaven,
that it was one of those signs,
railroad tracks just beyond.

When I told my hack-brother
at a dinner we relaxed over
for a few minutes, he roared,
half-choking on his burger,

"Welcome to the club, Bro.
What took you so long?"

# The Wrench

Other cabbies carried knives,
sawed-off bats, one hack kept
a .38:  disappointed he never got
to shoot a potential thief a line
Eastwood might've envied.

I never brought a weapon,
reasoned the Plexiglas shield
was safe enough:  not always true—
some fares paying through
the driver's open window, instead of
slipping the bills through the slot.

My Dad, when he was laid off,
came home late every night,
not just poker Thursdays.
One night a wrench fell from
the rolled up newspaper he carried
like a drum major's baton,
and clanged to our tiny
dining room's linoleum floor.

My mother screamed:  proof
he was hacking; my brother and I
stared, astounded our gentle father
was capable of using a weapon.

My feeling?  The job so shitty,
so exhausting in my going nowhere
for all the miles I logged,
that if someone wanted to kill me,

let him do it fast and put me
out of my misery.

# Just Drive Where She Tells You

The afternoon slow as the nags
my Dad bet on, I was stopped
at a light on the Upper East Side,
when my rear door startled open
like Belmont's starting gate.

A woman was shoved in;
she tried to say something,
but the man tossed me a C-note.

"Just drive her," he shouted,
"wherever she tells you!
And keep the change."
He vanished back into
a luxury apartment building.

Snatching the bill, I swiveled
for a destination; she sighed
an East Village walk-up address,
and closed her eyes.

At ride's end, I wanted to console,

"He's not worth it," and smile
sympathy at her pretty, tear-smudged
face, but didn't:  women's tears
the most terrifying force
I'd encountered in my young life.

# Loquacious

In fiction, cabbies are loquacious
as barbers, wise as bartenders.
In life, with few exceptions,
we drove stony as the Library's lions,
only not nearly as regal; we muttered
curses, figured the fastest routes,
so we could pick up the next ride,
and wondered how many more hours
and fares until we could clock out.

Besides, fares talked among themselves,
and if they were single passengers—
opinionated as crows and buzzards—
arguments could fly, so kiss
tips goodbye:  best to keep silent.

But once, I was humming a tune
by the Grateful Dead in that year
after my father died, and the passenger—
in a suit Gregory Peck or my Dad
might've envied—remarked.

"That's my favorite of their songs,"
and I couldn't shut up about the Dead,
and my own dead:  me the sad drinker,
he the wise and kind bartender-cabbie.

The ride over, he handed me a tip
my Dad would've called,

"New York-gangster generous."
I tried to hand it back, but he was gone.

The next fare barked an address
and route:  certain I'd cheat him.

# Robert Lowell in the Cab, II

I'd long escaped the screaming,
screeching, seething New York streets,
the day I read he'd died in a Manhattan cab.

I've always wondered if I'd the courage
to try CPR back then, or would've blasted
my horn, hoping a cop or doctor or nurse
would come to his, and my, rescue.

No one ever died in my cab, thank God,
but a couple performed the little death;
a junkie shot up; someone puked up
his St. Patrick's Day celebration;
and a couple smoked weed and made up
an excuse not to share, not that I would've,
on-duty, but it's always polite to ask.

But no one died in my cab; better,
I never killed anyone:  not other drivers
in a crash, not a passenger trying
to rip me off, not a pedestrian
not respecting how insane cabbies
could get when a light flashed green
and a potential fare waved a raised hand,
and three other hacks were primed
to take off like falcons snatching
pigeons out of the innocent sky.

Some nights, when rage rode beside me
like a hog-revving Angel crazed on speed,
I'd want to kneel in thanks at shift's end:

an image Lowell might've used in a poem
about confession, penitence, and gratitude
for all our little, doomed lives in America.

# The Last Night I Drove a Cab

There's a line in the horror movie, *Them*—
about giant radioactive ants in Arizona—
in which someone states that most murders
take place when the thermometer hits 92.
Above that evil degree, it's too hot to think
of lifting a weapon in rage; below, you're not
so clubbed by the heat that any stray word
demands lethal retribution.  But at deadly 92,
you're too hot and sweaty to consider
consequences and just enough energy
to smash someone over and over and over.

When I picked up my cab that afternoon,
it was exactly 92 degrees:  sun stabbing
with headache death-rays.  My first fare
shrieked, "The other corner!"  I shouted back,
"Get out, asshole!"  After that, I cursed at the fares
that had disappeared like in a sci-fi movie
about a cab driver who's thrust down to lonely hell.
I fantasized about driving the cab to Denver:
city of cowboys and gun racks, and the Creative
Writing program I'd start in a few weeks.

"Screw it," I finally muttered, the sun long set—
the temperature holding steady-vicious at 92—
and drove to the garage, hoping the dispatcher
would shout, "Cooperman, get back out
onto the street and earn me some more money!"
like he was my private pimp:  my excuse

to beat the crap out of him and drink his blood.

What he said was, "You missed your brother.
He left you this," and handed me a bag
with a salami sandwich and a package
of six of those tiny sugar-coated donuts, inside.
I wanted to apologize for hating Stan
like he was a Nazi butcher, wanted
to shake his hand goodbye, wish him
a good, sweet life; instead, I trudged out,
dreaming of cool, blue mountains.

# What Cabbies Knew

In movies and on TV
cabbies are wisecracking fonts
of all wisdom, dispensing advice
on everything, having seen it all.
In real life, we knew routes,
and about how much a fare might cost.

And unlike trucker lore,
we knew of no secret diners
to roll eyes in gastronomic ecstasies.
We just shoveled in food
like on Old West locomotives
desperate to outrun outlaws,
then back to our belching cabs.

We knew the hotels where fares
waited for rides to the airports,
or to restaurants, or the theatre,
and back again.  We knew when
Knicks and Rangers games ended,
and swooped down like eagles
to snatch fares to Brooklyn, the Bronx.
We knew when theatres closed,
classical and rock concerts ended.

You wanted advice?
Listen to your mother.
We drove, we just drove.

# About the Author

Robert Cooperman was born and raised in Brooklyn, N.Y., and earned a Ph.D. in Creative Writing from the University of Denver. He is the author of 14 previous poetry collections, most recently *Little Timothy in Heaven,* published by March Street Press; and *The Lily of the West*, brought out by Wind Publications. *In the Colorado Gold Fever Mountains* (Western Reflections Books) won the Colorado Book Award in 2000, and *The Widow's Burden* (Western Reflections Books) was runner-up for the WILLA Award from Women Writing the West. His work has appeared in *The American Poetry Review, The North American Review, Mississippi Review*, and *The Southern Humanities Review.* Cooperman lives in Denver with his wife Beth.

# Our Mission

The mission of Brick Road Poetry Press is to publish and promote poetry that entertains, amuses, edifies, and surprises a wide audience of appreciative readers. We are not qualified to judge who deserves to be published, so we concentrate on publishing what we enjoy. Our preference is for poetry geared toward dramatizing the human experience in language rich with sensory image and metaphor, recognizing that poetry can be, at one and the same time, both familiar as the perspiration of daily labor and as outrageous as a carnival sideshow.

# Also Available from Brick Road Poetry Press

www.brickroadpoetrypress.com

*Dancing on the Rim* by Clela Reed

*Possible Crocodiles* by Barry Marks

*Pain Diary* by Joseph D. Reich

*Otherness* by M. Ayodele Heath

*Drunken Robins* by David Oates

*Damnatio Memoriae* by Michael Meyerhofer

*Lotus Buffet* by Rupert Fike

*The Melancholy MBA* by Richard Donnelly

*Two-Star General* by Grey Held

*Chosen* by Toni Thomas

*Etch and Blur* by Jamie Thomas

*Water-Rites* by Ann E. Michael

*Bad Behavior* by Michael Steffen

*Tracing the Lines* by Susanna Lang

*Rising to the Rim* by Carol Tyx

*Treading Water with God* by Veronica Badowski

*Rich Man's Son* by Ron Self

# About the Prize

The Brick Road Poetry Prize, established in 2010, is awarded annually for the best book-length poetry manuscript. Entries are accepted August 1st through November 1st. The winner receives $1000 and publication. For details on our preferences and the complete submission guidelines, please visit our website at www.brickroadpoetrypress.com.

www.ingramcontent.com/pod-product-compliance
Lightning Source LLC
Chambersburg PA
CBHW031309060726
47590CB00003B/1130